DISCARD

D1217084

CHICAGO PUBLIC LIBRARY
THOMAS HUGHES CHILDRENS LIBRARY
400 S. STATE ST.   60605

Chickens/Gallinas

By JoAnn Early Macken

Reading Consultant: Jeanne Clidas, Ph.D.
Director, Roberts Wesleyan College Literacy Clinic

WEEKLY READER®
PUBLISHING

Please visit our web site at **www.garethstevens.com**.
For a free catalog describing our list of high-quality books,
call 1-877-542-2595 (USA) or 1-800-387-3178 (Canada).
Our fax: 1-877-542-2596

Library of Congress Cataloging-in-Publication Data

Macken, JoAnn Early, 1953–
    (Chickens. Spanish & English)
    Chickens = Gallinas / by JoAnn Early Macken.
       p. cm. — (Animals that live on the farm = Animales de la granja)
    Includes bibliographical references and index.
    ISBN-10: 1-4339-2427-7   ISBN-13: 978-1-4339-2427-9 (lib. bdg.)
    ISBN-10: 1-4339-2471-4   ISBN-13: 978-1-4339-2471-2 (soft cover)
    1. Chickens—Juvenile literature. I. Title. II. Title: Gallinas.
  SF487.5.M3312   2010
  636.5—dc22   2009011968

This edition first published in 2010 by
Weekly Reader® Books
An Imprint of Gareth Stevens Publishing
1 Reader's Digest Road
Pleasantville, NY 10570-7000 USA

Copyright © 2010 by Gareth Stevens, Inc.

Executive Managing Editor: Lisa M. Herrington
Senior Editor: Barbara Bakowski
Cover Designers: Jennifer Ryder-Talbot and Studio Montage
Production: Studio Montage
Translators: Tatiana Acosta and Guillermo Gutiérrez
Library Consultant: Carl Harvey, Library Media Specialist, Noblesville, Indiana

Photo credits: Cover, pp. 1, 7, 9, 11, 13, 17 Shutterstock; p. 5 © James P. Rowan; pp. 15, 19, 21 Gregg Andersen

All rights reserved. No part of this book may be reproduced, stored in a retrieval system,
or transmitted in any form or by any means, electronic, mechanical, photocopying, recording,
or otherwise, without the prior written permission of the copyright holder. For permission, contact
permissions@gspub.com.

Printed in the United States of America

1 2 3 4 5 6 7 8 9 14 13 12 11 10 09

Table of Contents

R0422644939
CHICAGO PUBLIC LIBRARY
THOMAS HUGHES CHILDRENS LIBRARY
400 S. STATE ST.   60605

- - - - - - - - - - - - - - -

Contenido

Boldface words appear in the glossary./
Las palabras en **negrita** aparecen en el glosario.

Baby Chickens

Peep! Peep! A baby chicken hatches from an egg. The baby chicken is called a **chick**.

- - - - - - - - - - - - - - - -

Pollitos

¡Pío! ¡Pío! Un **pollito** sale del cascarón. Los pollitos son las crías de las gallinas.

4

chicks/
pollitos

Chicks have fluffy yellow feathers. The feathers are called **down**.

- - - - - - - - - - - - -

Los pollitos tienen unas plumas esponjosas y amarillas llamadas **plumón**.

down/
plumón

Roosters and Hens

A grown female chicken is a **hen**. A grown male chicken is a **rooster**.

– – – – – – – – – – – – – – –

Gallos y gallinas

La **gallina** es una hembra adulta.
Un macho adulto es un **gallo**.

8

hen/
gallina

rooster/
gallo

9

On the farm, chickens live in small groups. During the day, they stay in the barnyard. They scratch and peck for food on the ground.

- - - - - - - - - - - - - - -

En la granja, las gallinas viven en grupos pequeños. Durante el día, se quedan en el corral. Escarban y picotean el suelo buscando comida.

Chickens eat seeds, plants, fruit, and berries. They also eat insects and worms.

- - - - - - - - - - - - - - -

Las gallinas se alimentan de semillas, plantas, frutas y bayas. También comen insectos y gusanos.

To drink, a chicken takes a sip of water.
It tilts its head back. The water runs down
its throat.

– – – – – – – – – – – – – –

Para beber, una gallina toma un sorbo
de agua e inclina la cabeza hacia atrás.
De esa forma, el agua le baja por la
garganta.

Chickens have feathers and wings. They cannot fly very far or high. Some chickens cannot fly at all!

- - - - - - - - - - - - - -

Las gallinas tienen plumas y alas. Sin embargo, no pueden volar muy alto ni muy lejos. ¡Algunas ni siquiera pueden hacerlo!

Life on the Farm

Many farmers keep chickens for eggs.
Chicken eggs can be white or brown.

- - - - - - - - - - - - - - -

La vida en la granja

Muchos granjeros crían gallinas por los
huevos. Los huevos pueden ser blancos
o marrones.

At night, the chickens stay inside a **coop**. There, they are safe from **predators**, such as foxes and hawks.

- - - - - - - - - - - - - -

Las gallinas pasan la noche en un **gallinero**. Allí están a salvo de **depredadores** como los zorros y los halcones.

Fast Facts/Datos básicos

Height/ Altura	about 30 inches (76 centimeters)/ unas 30 pulgadas (76 centímetros)
Wingspan/ Envergadura	about 28 inches (71 centimeters)/ unas 28 pulgadas (71 centímetros)
Weight/ Peso	about 7 pounds (3 kilograms)/ unas 7 libras (3 kilogramos)
Diet/ Dieta	seeds, plants, fruit, insects, and worms/semillas, plantas, fruta, insectos y gusanos
Average life span/ Promedio de vida	up to 7 years/ hasta 7 años

Glossary/Glosario

chick: a baby bird

coop: a small building or cage for chickens

down: soft, fluffy feathers

hen: a grown female chicken

predators: animals that kill and eat other animals

rooster: a grown male chicken

---

depredadores: animales que se comen a otros animales

gallina: hembra adulta

gallinero: edificación pequeña o jaula donde se crían gallinas

gallo: macho adulto

plumón: plumas suaves y esponjosas

pollito: cría de gallina

For More Information/Más información
Books/Libros
Animals at the Farm/Animales de la granja.
English-Spanish Foundations (series). Gladys Rosa-Mendoza
(me+mi publishing, 2004)

Chickens. Farm Animals (series). Robin Nelson (Lerner, 2009)

Web Sites/Páginas web
Flying Skunk Farm/Granja *Flying Skunk*
www.flyingskunk.com/live.html
Watch live video of the chickens at Flying Skunk Farm./
Miren videos en tiempo real de los pollos de la
granja *Flying Skunk.*

**Museum of Science and Industry: Baby Chicks Hatching/
Museo de las ciencias y la industria: Pollitos saliendo
del cascarón**
*www.msichicago.org/online-science/videos/video-detail/
activities/the-hatchery*
Watch a video of chicks hatching from eggs./Miren un video de
pollitos saliendo del cascarón.

Publisher's note to educators and parents: Our editors have carefully reviewed these web sites to ensure that they are suitable for children. Many web sites change frequently, however, and we cannot guarantee that a site's future contents will continue to meet our high standards of quality and educational value. Be advised that children should be closely supervised whenever they access the Internet.

Nota de la editorial a los padres y educadores: Nuestros editores han revisado con cuidado las páginas web para asegurarse de que son apropiadas para niños. Sin embargo, muchas páginas web cambian con frecuencia, y no podemos garantizar que sus contenidos futuros sigan conservando nuestros elevados estándares de calidad y de interés educativo. Tengan en cuenta que los niños deben ser supervisados atentamente siempre que accedan a Internet.

Index/Índice

About the Author

JoAnn Early Macken is the author of two rhyming picture books, *Sing-Along Song* and *Cats on Judy*, and more than 80 nonfiction books for children. Her poems have appeared in several children's magazines. She lives in Wisconsin with her husband and their two sons.

- - - - - - - - - - - - - - -

Información sobre la autora

JoAnn Early Macken ha escrito dos libros de rimas con ilustraciones, *Sing-Along Song* y *Cats on Judy*, y más de ochenta libros de no ficción para niños. Sus poemas han sido publicados en varias revistas infantiles. Vive en Wisconsin con su esposo y sus dos hijos.